FLOURISH.BANNER.FRAME.

555 ornaments and motifs for design and illustration

 dvd includes editable vector files, quick reference index and usage samples **VON GLITSCHKA**

HOW BOOKS

Cincinnati, Ohio
www.howdesign.com

Edited by Amy Owen
Designed by Grace Ring
Production coordinated by Greg Nock

TABLE OF CONTENTS

ABOUT THE AUTHOR

Von Glitschka has worked in the communication arts industry for over 23 years, and refers to himself as an "illustrative designer." In 2002, he started Glitschka Studios, a multidisciplinary creative firm.

His work reflects the symbiotic relationship between design and illustration; thus his modus operandi is that of a hired gun for both in-house art departments and medium to large creative agencies. He has worked on projects for clients such as Microsoft, Adobe, Pepsi, the Rock and Roll Hall of Fame, Major League Baseball, Hasbro, Wendy's, Bandai Toys, Allstate Insurance, Disney, Lifetime and HGTV.

His exuberant graphics have garnered numerous design and illustration awards and have appeared in such publications as *Communication Arts*, *PRINT*, *Graphis*, *American Illustration*, The Society of Illustrators annual, and *Logo Lounge 2, 3, 4, 5* and *6*.

He also operates the website IllustrationClass.com, where visitors can download tutorials documenting his illustrative design creative process on a variety of diverse project types.

He lives with his wife, two daughters, three cats, one frog and eight koi fish in the lovely Pacific Northwest in Oregon.

DEDICATION

My creative pursuits wouldn't be possible without the support and encouragement of my family and friends. The following people have taken the time to provide me with their insight, creativity and humor when I needed it the most, though they may not have realized it at the time. Thank you for helping me reach my dreams!

Dickie Adams	Amy Davis	Dave Hansen	Matt MacCollin
Jeff Andrews	Alyssa Glitschka	Randy Hill	John Nissen
Michael Bast	Becky Glitschka	Paul Howalt	Amy Owen
Ron Campbell	Savannah Glitschka	Scott Hull	Jeff Pollard

Note: All text in this book was tweaked and polished by Anastasia Soohoo-Hui. Thank you, Anastasia!

ART FOR ART

Ornament has adorned everything from humble chamber pots to everyday carpets to the sacred burial places of the dead. It has decorated tools as rudimentary as hand axes and whole buildings as majestic as palaces. As long as art itself has existed, so has ornament.

Even as recently as a hundred years ago, ornament was everywhere. Now skip forward to present day—and it seems like you must strain to find it. For nearly a hundred years, art and craft have avoided ornament like the plague. It is not because we are afraid of making something too beautiful, but rather we have changed our definition of what is aesthetically pleasing.

Since the boom of machinery and mass production, we have become enamored with what art historian James Trilling calls "the beauty of the necessary." Functionality and practicality of design are to us what complex decoration and ornamentation were to people that lived in almost any other era. Instead of curlicues and flourishes, we prefer straight, efficient lines. Instead of whimsy, we want dependability. Perhaps nothing illustrates this so well as the popularity of the Swedish furniture store IKEA. IKEA is a company built around the concept of frugality—not in cost alone, but in design too. Their product line specializes in the functional and inexpensive. No materials or money are to be wasted on time-consuming artisanship and decoration. The result? A very modern, austere look that lends itself superbly to organization, rearrangement and daily use—all good, functional qualities. But it's also a look that, without ornament to let your eyes wander freely, may starve your sense of beauty and repose after a while.

This need for functionality is compounded by the effects of the technological advances of the past few decades. Now, not only do we want practicality for our design, we must have efficiency as well. This desire is reflected in our approach to web design, and probably rightly so. Our experience with the World Wide Web has taught us to expect a much faster pace online than in face-to-face life. In "Internet time," we expect to absorb the information we want much more quickly. If we cannot find what we're looking for within a few clicks on a website, we judge it poorly designed—never mind how "nice" it looks. The standard of efficiency can be useful when applied to accessing specific information, but when applied to art, it's self defeating. We don't enjoy a painting or sculpture for how quickly we can look at it; we enjoy it for *how* it tells us what it is.

Ornament may currently be a bit overshadowed by functionality and efficiency, but an art that has existed since the beginning of time will not cease to exist simply because it's not practiced in every corner. People may shift preferences every so often, but the need for art never changes.

In a culture obsessed with function and end, ornament reminds us that form and means are equally important. A work infused with ornament compels us to take a longer look to appreciate the force and complexity of the idea behind it. Let's face it—even art needs art sometimes. Without it, we may be left with a purely functional piece that does its job communicating its content, but not much else.

Regardless of what the nearest thesaurus may imply about ornament being a "frill," "frou-frou," "bauble," or "doodad," its purpose is important. Even the simplest border can add a complex effect to a design. Flourishes and frames give us a context for the content of what we see. If used well, ornament magnifies the impact of the design for the beholder; it will be integrated seamlessly into the rest of the artwork. As the famous architect Frank Lloyd Wright put it, "True ornament is not a matter of prettifying externals. It is organic with the structure it adorns, whether a person, a building, or a park."

Besides decoration, ornament also serves as the primary way of visualizing a motif in art. Motif, as design within design, provides a kind of spatial rhythm to a piece. It details the feelings behind the work, perhaps conveying a deeper emotion the artist wants us to experience.

Motif is essential to the storytelling aspect of any art, be it musical, literary, or visual. In music, a motif is usually represented by a short phrase repeated throughout the song. Sometimes it may vary the key, the tempo, the rhythm or even a few of the notes, but it is still there, and still recognizable. In literature, a motif may be a recurring literary device or idea. Different characters may participate, and different symbols may be used, but the same idea surrounds them. So, though we may not recall every single note of *Beethoven's Fifth*, or each death metaphor in *Hamlet*, we will remember the apprehension invoked by three short notes and a long one, or the revulsion elicited by a man talking to a skull ("Alas, poor Yorick…").

The purpose of motif across the disciplines is to convey a central idea that the work is built around. In visual art it's much the same with repetition and structure, just with slightly different devices. But in the visual arts, ornament and motif are so closely bound they are nearly indistinguishable from one other. The recurrence of a symbol or pattern unifies and strengthens that main idea, driving it into our hearts and minds. Motifs define style and identify themes. The ancient Celts incorporated plant, animal and figure ornamentation interwoven together, representing the connectedness of their mythology. The abstract motifs prevalent in Islamic art reveal their passion for math and geometry.

Certainly ornament serves a higher purpose than "mere" decoration. It identifies, unifies, beautifies, even glorifies. But I believe there is a higher purpose still: It pleases us. No amount of analyzing or examination can tell us *why*—but we love it. When it comes down to it, we like ornament because it is beautiful, and we like beauty. Indeed, if pleasure were not at its core, would we continue to love it? Perhaps this is why the artist John Ruskin said, "I believe the right question to ask, respecting all ornament, is simply this; was it done with enjoyment, was the carver happy while he was about it?"

Von has put together this resource of decorative art to be used and enjoyed by illustrators and designers alike. I hope it delights you as much as it did me.

—ANASTASIA SOOHOO-HUI

INTRODUCTION

A DECORATED DESIGNER

"Design is more than decoration."

The essence of that statement rings true. Especially in the context of a consumer-driven industry that depends on diverse marketing strategies, decoration is essential in order to be viable in an ever-changing landscape of competing brand messages.

Decoration has its place firmly rooted in history. One need only study the past to find a profusion of examples: Egyptian artifacts that show a foliage ornament geometrically arranged within a frieze, Assyrian lotus ornaments gracing parts of an ancient throne, Greek plates displaying patterned borders, Roman columns with Corinthian capitals, the illuminated manuscript printed in the Gutenberg Bible, or the beautiful decorative tapestries of William Morris.

It's obvious that history is replete with mankind's fascination regarding all things decorative. Creative-minded people enjoy using beautifully decorative elements within their work, and rightly so. But our challenge is to balance the use of ornaments appropriately within our work, because design is more than decoration.

One of my favorite quotes about art sums up this creative balance well;

"WHEN I AM WORKING ON A PROBLEM, I NEVER THINK ABOUT BEAUTY. I ONLY THINK ABOUT HOW TO SOLVE THE PROBLEM. BUT WHEN I HAVE FINISHED, IF THE SOLUTION IS NOT BEAUTIFUL, I KNOW IT IS WRONG."
—R. Buckminster Fuller

My motivation behind this volume of original ornamentation, flourishes, borders, frames, etc., is to provide a digital resource of well-crafted, elegant and creative motifs a graphic designer or illustrator could use to beautify and enhance his or her own design work.

It's my hope you find this book useful, inspiring and informative.

—VON GLITSCHKA

NOTE FROM THE AUTHOR: Can't find an ornament that works for you? Glitschka Studios can create an original design motif specifically for your project. Contact us directly at von@glitschka.com.

FEATURED ARTIST: ROB McCLURKAN

Illustrator | Atlanta, Georgia, USA | www.seerobdraw.com

Image used: FLOR91

When I first laid eyes on this whimsical branch frame, I was immediately swept to a land far away, a place where upon first glance all I saw was lush greenery holding tightly to thick vines as they twist and turn. Just beyond the branches became the perfect spot for a tiny cottage to rest. I used the pattern to evoke a feeling of enchantment.

ONCE UPON A TIME. Artwork created by Rob McClurkan. Copyright © 2010.

2

BANNERS

Your creative projects will have a banner year using the diverse assortment of wrapped, swirling, twisted and arched banner motifs.

BAN1

BAN2

BAN3

BAN4

BAN5

BAN6

BAN7

BAN8

BAN9

BAN10

BAN11

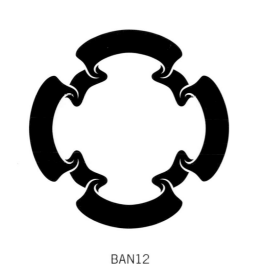

BAN12

BAN13

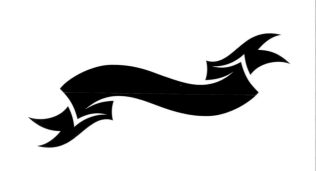

BAN14

BAN15

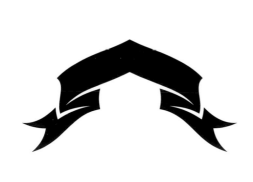

BAN16

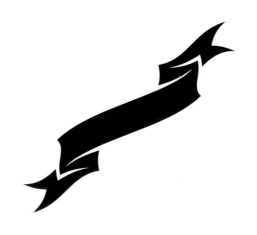

BAN17

BAN18

BAN19

BAN20

BAN21

BAN22

BAN23

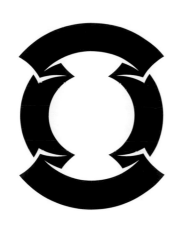

BAN24

BAN25

BAN26

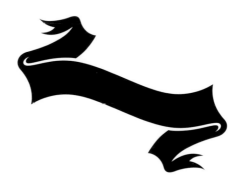

BAN27

BAN28

BAN29

FEATURED ARTIST: JUSTIN AHRENS

Creative Director | Geneva, Illinois, USA | www.rule29.com

Image used: FRAM32

This art reminded me of the hazards and constant restrictions that the kids I was privileged to meet in the slums of Kenya face daily. They need to believe their lives are bigger than what is all around them and find the good in their daily lives. The juxtaposition of the graphic, the type and the image represent the struggle between good and evil, as well as the strength and change of direction that can happen with a simple shift of perspective.

BELIEVE. Artwork created by Justin Ahrens. Copyright © 2010.

BORDERS

Secure your graphic border with these unique motifs. They can seamlessly span the distance of your design or enhance an edge of your layout.

BORD1

BORD2

BORD3

BORD4

BORD5

BORD6

BORD7

BORD8

BORD9

BORD10

BORD11

BORD12

BORD13

BORD14

BORD15

BORD16

BORD17

BORD18

BORD19

BORD20

BORD21

BORD22

BORD23

BORD24

BORD25

BORD26

BORD27

BORD28

BORD29

BORD30

BORD31

BORD32

BORD33

BORD34

BORD35

BORD36

BORD37

BORD38

BORD39

BORD40

BORD41

BORD42

BORD43

BORD44

BORD45

BORD46

BORD47

FEATURED ARTIST: JULIA-ANNE BORK

Graphic Designer | Seattle, Washington, USA | www.mint-usa.com

Image used: RING4

Winged bull: Adios to the ancients.

GOODBYE BABYLON. Artwork created by Julia-Anne Bork. Copyright © 2010.

CORNER TREATMENTS

Don't make your design go sit in the corner like a graphic dunce—dress up your boring corners with this collection of creative imagery.

COR1

COR2

COR3

COR4

COR5

COR6

COR7

COR8

COR9

COR10

COR11

COR12

COR13

COR14

COR15

COR16

COR17

COR18

COR19

COR20

COR21

COR22

COR23

COR24

COR25

COR26

COR27

COR28

COR29

COR30

COR31

COR32

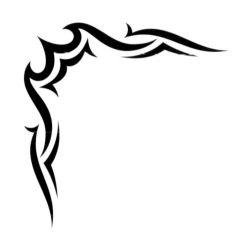

COR33

COR34

COR35

COR36

COR37

COR38

COR39

COR40

COR41

COR42

COR43

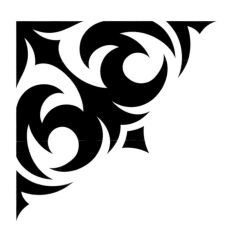

COR44

COR45

COR46

COR47

COR48

COR49

COR50

COR51

COR52

COR53

FEATURED ARTIST: JOHN MARTZ

Illustrator | Toronto, Ontario, Canada | www.johnmartz.com

Image used: BORD12

It was clear to me that this blobby shape needed to be turned into a sloppy, gushing stream of some sort, but I also didn't want to go gross. So ketchup and mustard it was. Matching the illustration style to the given artwork was an additional challenge, requiring me to dust off my vector hat.

MAIN SQUEEZE. Artwork created by John Martz. Copyright © 2010.

FLORAL & FLOURISHES

Experience the "frill" of creative victory, while avoiding the agony of design defeat with these graceful graphics and beautified curves.

FLOR1

FLOR2

FLOR3

FLOR4

FLOR5

FLOR6

FLOR7

FLOR8

FLOR9

FLOR10

FLOR11

FLOR12

FLOR13

FLOR14

FLOR15

FLOR16

FLOR17

FLOR18

FLOR19

FLOR20

FLOR21

FLOR22

FLOR23

FLOR24

FLOR25

FLOR26

FLOR27

FLOR28

FLOR29

FLOR30

FLOR31

FLOR32

FLOR33

FLOR34

FLOR35

FLOR36

FLOR37

FLOR38

FLOR39

FLOR40

FLOR41

FLOR42

FLOR43

FLOR44

FLOR45

FLOR46

FLOR47

FLOR48

FLOR49

FLOR50

FLOR51

FLOR52

FLOR53

FLOR54

FLOR55

FLOR56

FLOR57

FLOR58

FLOR59

FLOR60

FLOR61

FLOR62

FLOR63

FLOR64

FLOR65

FLOR66

FLOR67

FLOR68

FLOR69

FLOR70

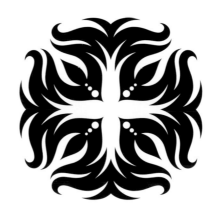

FLOR71

FLOR72

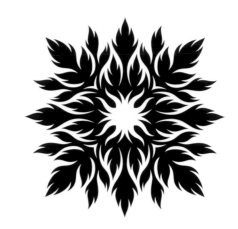

FLOR73

FLOR74

FLOR75

FLOR76

FLOR77

FLOR78

FLOR79

FLOR80

FLOR81

FLOR82

FLOR83

FLOR84

FLOR85

FLOR86

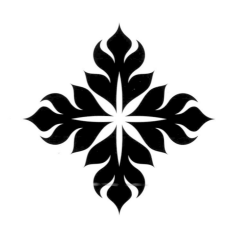

FLOR87

FLOR88

FLOR89

FLOR90

FLOR91

FLOR92

FLOR93

FLOR94

FLOR95

FEATURED ARTIST: U! CREATIVE TEAM

Miamisburg, Ohio, USA I www.ucreate.us

Image used: FLOR47

Beloved Virus is a line of Christian apparel that is designed to appeal to a wide audience, many of whom will discover the real meaning hidden within the design only after they read the hang tag or visit the site at www.belovedvirus.com.

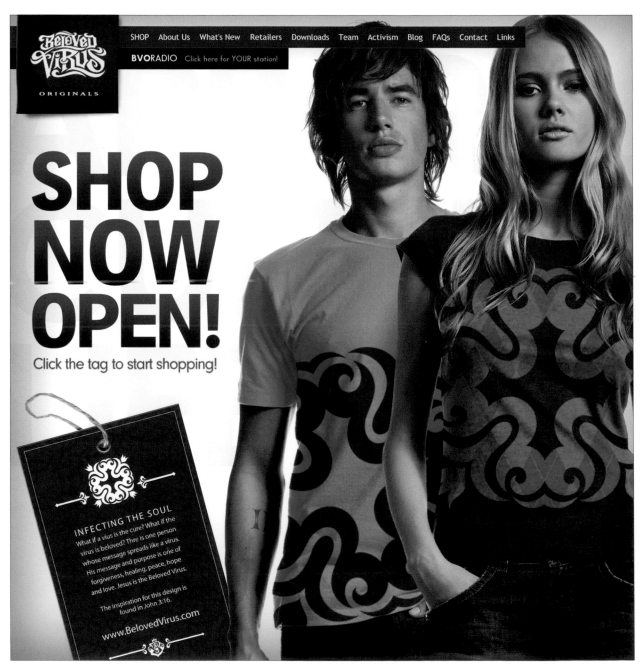

BELOVED VIRUS ORIGINALS. Design created by U! Creative. Copyright © 2010.

FRAMES

Use this selection of unique creative motifs to put you in the right frame of mind for your next design project.

FRAM1

FRAM2

FRAM3

FRAM4

FRAM5

FRAM6

FRAM7

FRAM8

FRAM9

FRAM10

FRAM11

FRAM12

FRAM13

FRAM14

FRAM15

FRAM16

FRAM17

FRAM18

FRAM19

FRAM20

FRAM21

FRAM22

FRAM23

FRAM24

FRAM25

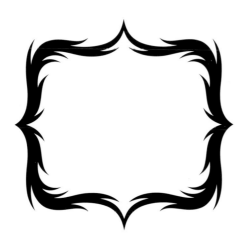

FRAM26

FRAM27

FRAM28

FRAM29

FRAM30

FRAM31

FRAM32

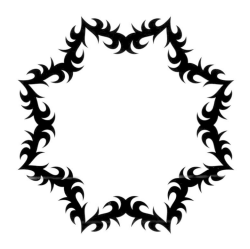

FRAM33

FRAM34

FRAM35

FRAM36

FRAM37

FRAM38

FRAM39

FRAM40

FRAM41

FRAM42

FRAM43

FRAM44

FRAM45

FRAM46

FRAM47

FRAM48

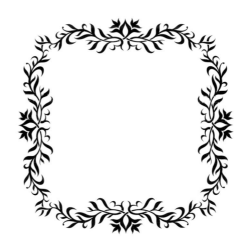

FRAM49

FRAM50

FRAM51

FRAM52

FRAM53

FRAM54

FRAM55

FRAM56

FRAM57

FRAM58

FRAM59

FRAM60

FRAM61

FRAM62

FRAM63

FRAM64

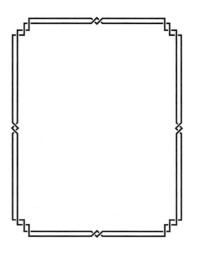

FRAM65

FRAM66

FRAM67

FRAM68

FRAM69

FRAM70

FRAM71

FRAM72

FRAM73

FRAM74

FRAM75

FRAM76

FRAM77

FRAM78

FRAM79

FRAM80

FRAM81

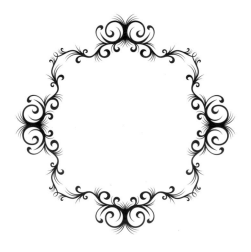

FRAM82

FRAM83

FRAM84

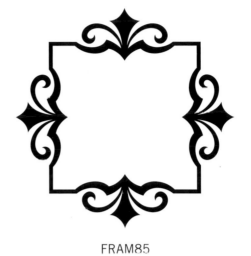

FRAM85

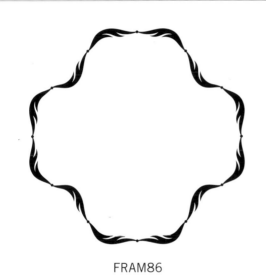

FRAM86

FRAM87

FRAM88

FRAM89

FRAM90

FRAM91

FRAM92

FRAM93

FRAM94

FRAM95

FRAM96

FRAM97

FRAM98

FRAM99

FRAM100

FRAM101

FEATURED ARTIST: MEG HUNT

Illustrator I Portland, Oregon, USA I www.meghunt.com

Image used: ORN44

When I received the ornament, the first thing that came to mind were flowers and flames, which brought to mind growth. So I decided to portray a girl surrounded by flowers, and implement the ornament as a texture as well as a glowing mark upon her head.

THE AWAKENING. Artwork created by Meg Hunt. Copyright © 2010.

GRAPHIC RINGS

Is your circular design feeling like Dante's *Inferno*? These heavenly graphics will be your creative redemption.

RING1

RING2

RING3

RING4

RING5

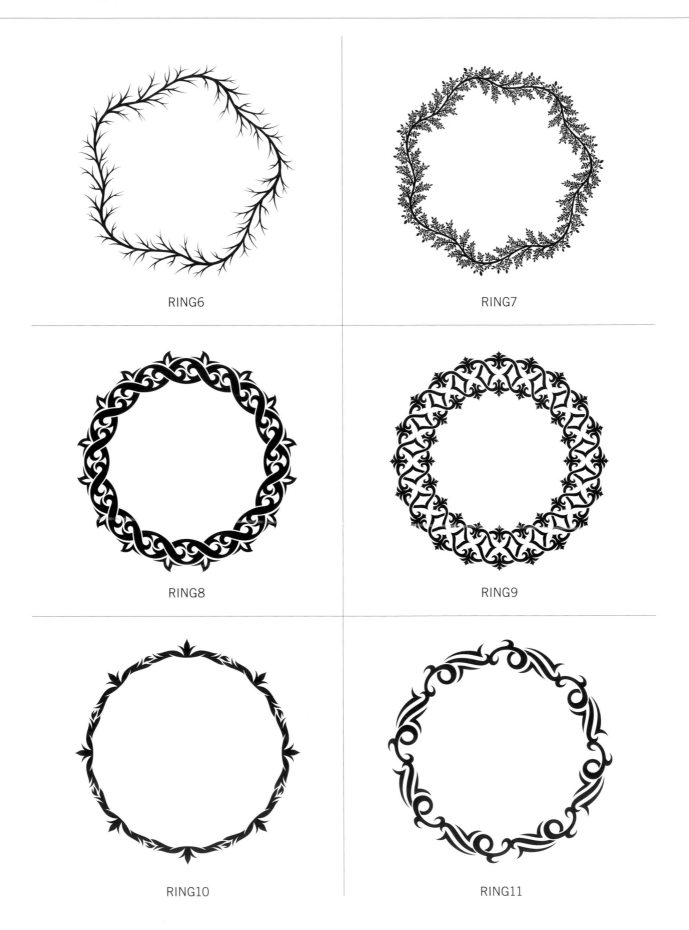

RING6

RING7

RING8

RING9

RING10

RING11

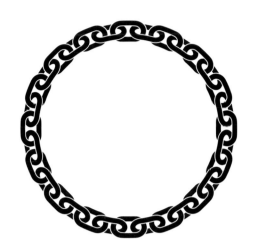

RING12

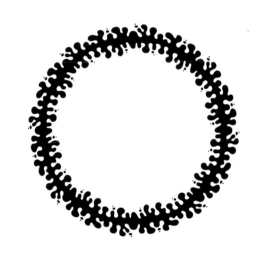

RING14

RING16

RING13

RING15

RING17

RING18

RING19

RING20

RING21

RING22

RING23

RING24

RING25

RING26

RING27

RING28

RING29

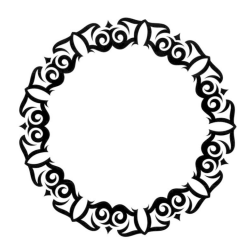

RING30

RING31

RING32

RING33

RING34

RING35

RING36

RING37

RING38

RING39

RING40

RING41

RING42

RING43

RING44

RING45

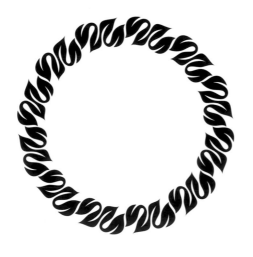

RING46

RING47

RING48

RING49

RING50

RING51

RING52

RING53

RING54

RING55

RING56

RING57

RING58

RING59

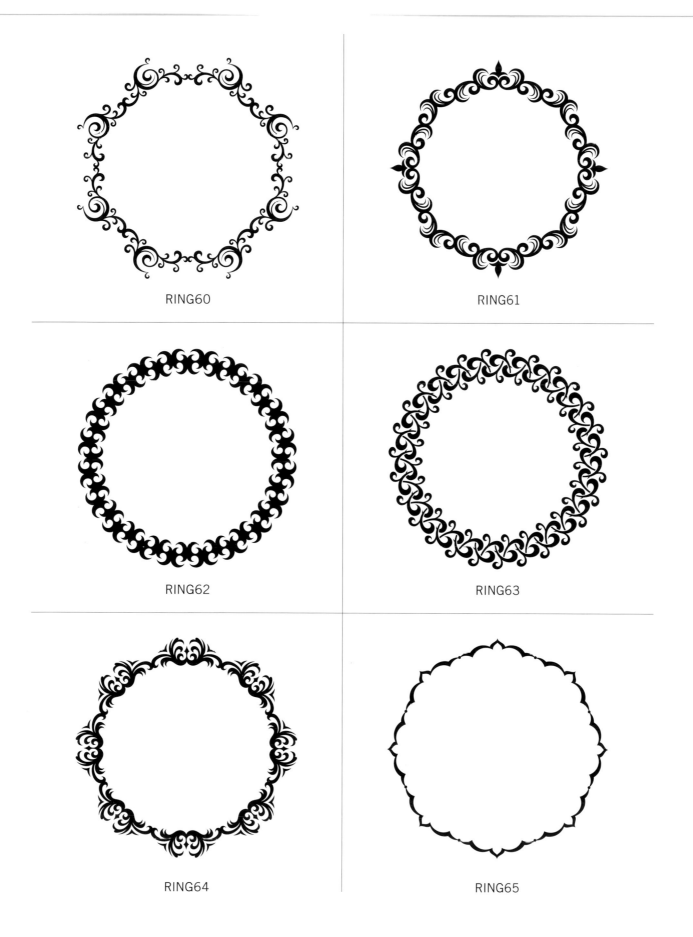

RING60

RING61

RING62

RING63

RING64

RING65

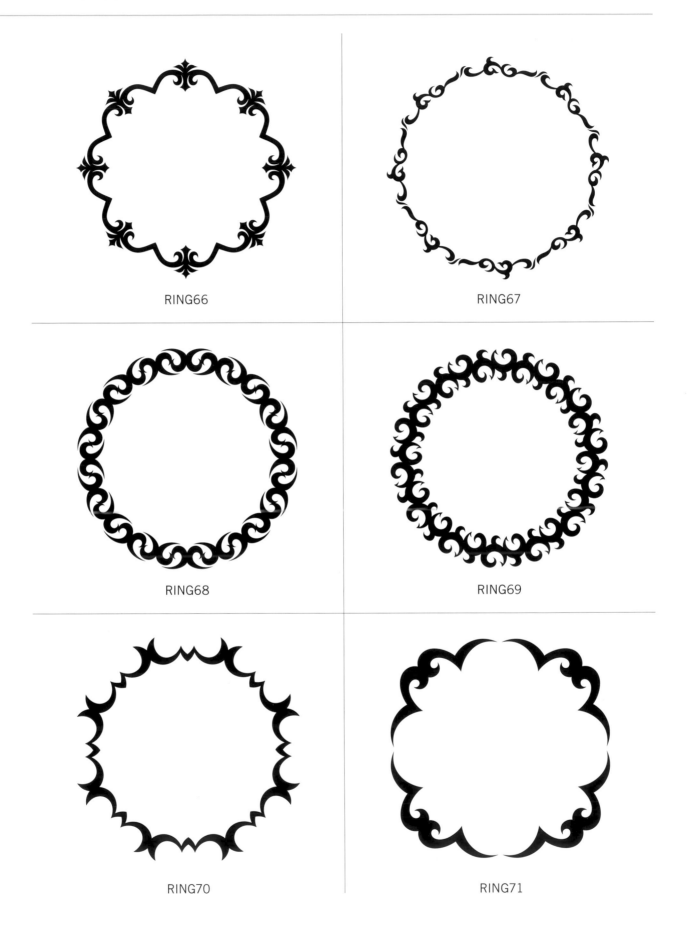

RING66

RING67

RING68

RING69

RING70

RING71

FEATURED ARTIST: GREG EPKES

Illustrator | Portland, Oregon, USA | www.epkes.com

Image used: FLOR18

Jolly Santa Claus is the product of multiple doodles and sketches I did while waiting in the car and various other places. I finished it in Adobe Illustrator, using the Shape tools and the Pathfinder tool for subtraction.

JOLLY SANTA. Artwork created by Greg Epkes. Copyright © 2010.

ORNAMENTS

As a professional designer, you'll be able to masterfully infuse your creative projects with these elegant embellishments.

ORN1

ORN2

ORN3

ORN4

ORN5

ORN6

ORN7

ORN8

ORN9

ORN10

ORN11

ORN12

ORN13

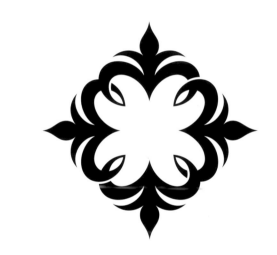

ORN14

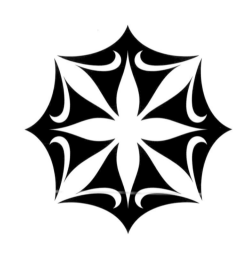

ORN15

ORN16

ORN17

ORN18

ORN19

ORN20

ORN21

ORN22

ORN23

ORN24

ORN25

ORN26

ORN27

ORN28

ORN29

ORN30

ORN31

ORN32

ORN33

ORN34

ORN35

ORN36

ORN37

ORN38

ORN39

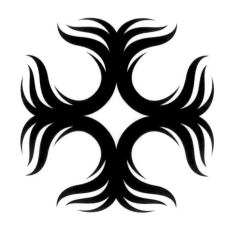

ORN40

ORN41

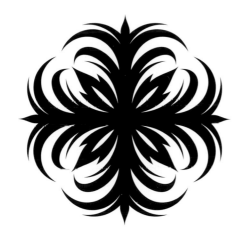

ORN42

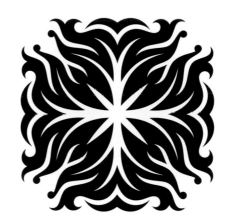

ORN43

ORN44

ORN45

ORN46

ORN47

ORN48

ORN49

ORN50

ORN51

ORN52

ORN53

ORN54

ORN55

ORN56

ORN57

ORN58

ORN59

ORN60

ORN61

ORN62

ORN63

ORN64

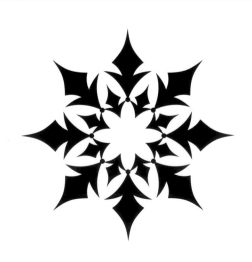

ORN65

ORN66

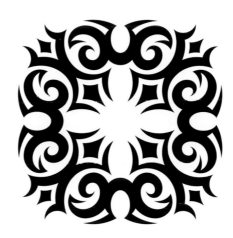

ORN67

ORN68

ORN69

ORN70

ORN71

ORN72

ORN73

ORN74

ORN75

ORN76

ORN77

ORN78

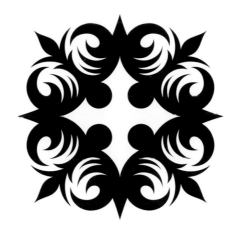

ORN79

ORN80

ORN81

ORN82

ORN83

ORN84

ORN85

ORN86

ORN87

ORN88

ORN89

ORN90

ORN91

ORN92

ORN93

ORN94

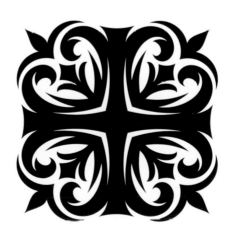

ORN95

FEATURED ARTIST: EARL GEE

Creative Director | San Francisco, California, USA | www.geechungdesign.com

Image used: FLOR72

The "Perennial" ornament embodies the timeless themes of ambition and power central to Shakespeare's *MacBeth*. MacBeth's ambition compels him to spill the blood of rival royal heirs and doom his own fate, symbolized by the blood-red shadow he casts. Birnam Wood lurks in the background, while the fog creates a metaphor for MacBeth's state of mind. Lady Mac-Beth agonizes over her actions in the famous hand-washing scene.

MACBETH POSTER. Design created by Earl Gee. Copyright © 2010.

PLACARDS & CARTOUCHES

Every design needs a solid creative foundation. With this collection of diverse backgrounds, you'll be able to solidify a great solution.

PLAC1

PLAC2

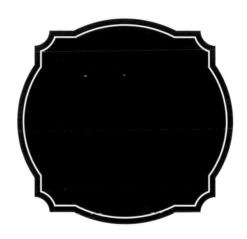

PLAC3

PLAC4

PLAC5

PLAC6

PLAC7

PLAC8

PLAC9

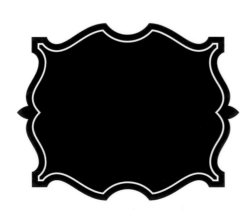

PLAC10

PLAC11

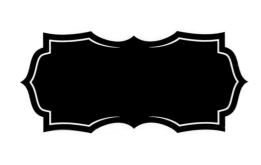

PLAC12

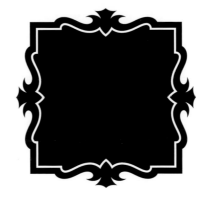

PLAC13

PLAC14

PLAC15

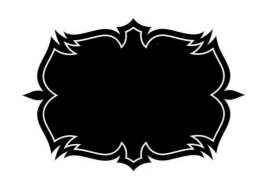

PLAC16

PLAC17

PLAC18

PLAC19

PLAC20

PLAC21

PLAC22

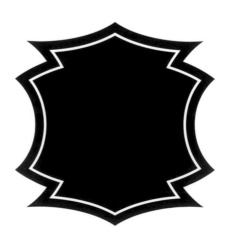

PLAC23

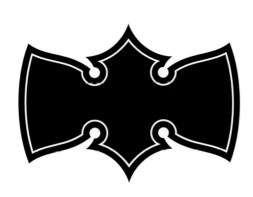

PLAC24

PLAC25

PLAC26

PLAC27

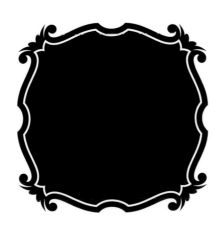

PLAC28

PLAC29

FEATURED ARTIST: JARED CHAPMAN

Illustrator | Ottawa, Ontario, Canada | www.jaredchapman.com

Image used: ORN49

When I saw the ornament I'd be working with, I immediately thought of the Middle Ages, specifically the Crusades. I originally intended to pair the pattern with a knight, but one idea evolved into another, and when it was all said and done, this is what I had.

KING BEAT. Artwork created by Jared Chapman. Copyright © 2010.

TRIBAL FLAIR

Don't be coy with your creativity. Take some risks, be a rebel, and tattoo your design with these bad-ass motifs.

TRIB1

TRIB2

TRIB3

TRIB4

TRIB5

TRIB6

TRIB7

TRIB8

TRIB9

TRIB10

TRIB11

TRIB12

TRIB13

TRIB14

TRIB15

TRIB16

TRIB17

TRIB18

TRIB19

TRIB20

TRIB21

TRIB22

TRIB23

TRIB24

TRIB25

TRIB26

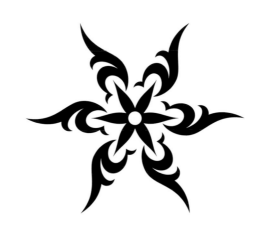

TRIB27

TRIB28

TRIB29

TRIB30

TRIB31

TRIB32

TRIB33

TRIB34

TRIB35

FEATURED ARTIST: JIM PAILLOT

Illustrator | Gilbert, Arizona, USA | www.jimpaillot.com

Image used: TRIB4

Pilates, a walk to the beach and then back to an unfinished crossword puzzle—snack cakes know how to keep it simple. They are injected with a sweet, creamy mixture of happiness and karma and then fortified with the most powerful artificial preservatives science can produce. They give back by sharing their advances in surfing, macrame and neck hickeys.

SURF SHACK. Artwork created by Jim Paillot. Copyright © 2010.

60 Stunning Textures for Design and Illustration

Crumble Crackle Burn features 60 photographic textures of natural, real-world surfaces, along with corresponding examples of how they can be applied in design and illustration projects. The companion DVD contains over 120 high-resolution texture images (the 60 in the book plus 60 bonus textures) that are ready for professional use. These organic textures are timeless in application and will quickly become a favorite resource.

94 Incredible Patterns for Design and Illustration

Drip Dot Swirl is an amazing library that contains 94 original vector patterns. Styles range from intricate knotwork to subtle florals to retro wallpaper to alien-inspired mazes. With examples from ten artists, you'll see how top designers and illustrators use the patterns in various projects. Includes DVD with all the patterns in the book, as well as 12 bonus patterns.

FIND THESE BOOKS AND MANY OTHERS AT MYDESIGNSHOP.COM OR YOUR LOCAL BOOKSTORE.